WHAT THE BIBLE SAYS I HAVE

JAKE & KEITH PROVANCE

I HAVE What the Bible Says I have
ISBN: 978-1-936314-08-9
Copyright © 2018 by Word and Spirit Publishing

Published by Word and Spirit Publishing
P.O. Box 701403
Tulsa, Oklahoma 74170

Contents

About the Authors

Keith Provance, involved in Christian publishing for more than 30 years, is the founder and president of Word and Spirit Publishing, a company dedicated to the publishing and worldwide distribution of scriptural, life-changing books. He also works as a publishing consultant to national and international ministries. Keith continues to write with his wife and with his son Jake. He and his wife, Megan, have authored a number of bestselling books with total sales of over 2 million copies. They reside in Tulsa, Oklahoma and are the parents of three sons, Ryan, Garrett, and Jake.

You may contact Keith at
Keith@WordAndSpiritPublishing.com

Jake Provance is an avid reader and an aspiring young writer, who has written five books and has plans to write several more. Jake's first book, Keep Calm & Trust God, has sold more than 500,000 copies. Jake is a graduate of Domata Bible School in Tulsa, OK, and has a call on his life to work in pastoral care ministry, with a particular passion to minister to young adults. Jake and his wife, Leah, live in Tulsa, OK.

Check out Jake's blog at Life-Speak.com

You may contact Jake at
Jake@WordAndSpiritPublishing.com

Introduction

Many Christians walk through life woefully unaware of the arsenal of God's gifts that they have at their disposal. The Bible tells us that when we accept Jesus as our Savior, we are adopted into God's family. God becomes our Father, and as His children we gain access to all our loving Father has to offer.

God is not ignorant of the pressures, problems, and temptations that we all face. That is why God has given you His support and the equipment you need to rise above every issue that arises in your life. All of His gifts are already yours! You don't have to sacrifice anything to obtain them, you don't have to live a perfect life to earn them, and you don't have to work really hard to be worthy of them. All you have to do is accept them just as you are.

God gave us life so that He could have children to love and spend time with. He has given us a purpose to accomplish so that we know that we are important and unique to Him. He gave us hope so that no matter how tragic life seems, we can know He is by our side and will help us get through any crisis. He gave us grace so that nothing could come between Him and His kids. He placed Jesus at His right hand, giving Him the position as our Advocate so that Jesus can relay our heart to the Father with perfect accuracy.

God gave us His protection so that we can walk confidently in obedience with him without fear. He gave us supernatural peace that passes all human understanding so we can navigate the tumultuous waters of this life with confidence and a triumphant spirit. He gave us authority and dominion to walk as His ambassadors on this earth. He has given us His provision so we will have all that we need—and plenty more to achieve our destiny and bless multitudes of people along the way. He gave us the promise of healing so that we would not live in hurt and pain or be stopped from accomplishing our mission on this earth. He gave us wisdom for all of life's decisions. He gave us faith and victory to overcome any trial, and He gave us a way out so that we are never at the mercy of our circumstances.

Jesus' sacrifice bought us back from destruction, and now we have a position of prominence with the Father. God gave us a position in His kingdom, a way of living on this earth as our inheritance just because we belong to him. He gave us His Spirit, to reside in us and to convey the truths of His Word and His love to us. He is our Guide, Mentor, and Counselor, and He empowers us with the same resurrection power that raised Christ Jesus from the dead so that we can triumph over any situation with the spirit of a conqueror.

And this is only scratching the surface. God's gifts are waiting for you! All you need to do is to reach out and grab them and operate in His divine strength, peace, and joy.

Chapter 1

I Have a Father

When you accepted Jesus as your personal Savior, the Bible says that you become part of God's family, a child of God. God became your Father!

Jesus' main purpose in coming to the earth was to connect God's kids back with Him—not just a superficial relationship but a close and intimate connection with your Father. We tend to overcomplicate what it means to be a Christian, but when you boil the Christian message down you get a very simple truth:

We were created in the likeness of God *because God wanted children,* and when humanity messed up, He valued us so much that He sent Jesus to die to buy His children back.

When Jesus was on earth, He referred to God as "Abba," which translates in our modern language to "Daddy." It's an intimate name for father that we can now call Him. When you need help with a problem or you simply need a friend, you have your Daddy to talk to.

He cares for you, loves you, and wants a close relationship with you. He wants to spend time with you, to walk through life with you, to laugh with you, and to be a shoulder for you to cry on. He wants to protect you from any danger. He wants to give you Fatherly advice and help you make the right decision. He wants you to be happy, at peace, and flourishing in whatever you do.

He knows the number of hairs on your head, He knit you together in the womb, and He knew you and loved you even before you breathed your first breath. He is your Daddy—there is no mistake He can't forgive, there is no sickness He can't heal, and there is no situation that He can't solve. He gave you His Spirit, and a guidebook we call the Bible, to help you navigate through the tumultuous waters of everyday life. So, run to your Father with your problems, with your mistakes, and with all your insecurities, because He loves you unconditionally and wants you to enjoy your life as His child.

Scriptures

But for us, There is one God, the Father, by whom all things were created, and for whom we live. And there is one Lord, Jesus Christ, through whom all things were created, and through whom we live.

–1 Corinthians 8:6 (NLT)

See what kind of love the Father has given to us, that we should be called children of God; and so we are. The reason why the world does not know us is that it did not know him.

–1 John 3:1 (ESV)

And you did not receive the "spirit of religious duty," leading you back into the fear *of never being good enough.* But you have received the "Spirit of full acceptance," enfolding you into the family of God. And you will never feel orphaned, for as he rises up within us, our spirits join him in saying the words of tender affection, "Beloved Father!"

–Romans 8:15 (TPT)

Speak These Words Over Your Life

I am a child of God, God is my heavenly Father. I have a solid connection, an untouchable bond, and a relationship that cannot diminish with Him. My Father loves me unconditionally, and there is nothing that can separate me from His love. It knows no bounds. He forgives me of all my sins. His love and grace fill my heart with fullness of joy. He loves me in spite of my shortcoming and inadequacies. My reliance on my Father God gets me through the day, causes me to overcome every adverse circumstance that I face, and gives me the confidence, courage, and ability to achieve greatness. It is my reliance on my Father God that sets me apart and gives me exactly what I need to accomplish every task that I am assigned. My Father has displayed His love for me in a way that will cause me never to doubt His willingness or His ability to come through for me. So, I boldly declare that My God is my Father and I will live my life for Him.

Chapter 2

I Have a Purpose and a Destiny

We all have had hopes and dreams of accomplishing something significant in our lives, but as we grow older those dreams and desires are shoved to the back of our minds as the responsibilities, obligations, and the demands of life begin to take their place.

You may feel as though you have wasted too much time and let your opportunity pass you by. You may feel that greatness is simply not in the cards for you anymore, but there is good news for you. God has a history of using imperfect people to accomplish great things. So regardless of time wasted or sins committed, regardless of your numerous responsibilities or obligations, regardless of any insecurities or hopelessness you may experience, GOD STILL PICKS YOU.

You have a purpose; you have a destiny. There is a task that no one else can accomplish the way God meant it to be accomplished except you. There is a place that you will flourish. There is a future of fulfillment and contentment ahead of you. You don't have to know how—or even what—all you have to do is open up your heart and be willing to follow God's plan and destiny for your life.

Many worry about what their destiny and purpose is exactly. They want to please God but have no idea where to start. The Bible says when you seek after God, you will find Him, and when you draw near to God, He will draw near to you. When you draw close to God and seek His will, a beautiful moment occurs as the weight in your life melts away as He teaches you how to live freely and lightly. God will reveal His plan and destiny for your life as you honor Him with your time, read His words, speak His words over your life, worship Him, and by praying to Him, laying your whole heart before Him. With your eyes fixed on God chasing after Him with all your heart, you'll find yourself right in the middle of your destiny.

Scriptures

"For I know the plans I have for you," declares the Lord, "plans to prosper you and not to harm you, plans to give you hope and a future."

–JEREMIAH 29:11 (NIV)

"*I pray with great faith for you,* because I'm fully convinced that the One who began this glorious work in you will faithfully continue the process of maturing you and will put his finishing touches to it until the unveiling of our Lord Jesus Christ!"

–PHILIPPIANS 1:6 (TPT)

"For those whom He foreknew and loved and chose beforehand, He also predestined to be conformed to the image of His Son and ultimately share in His complete sanctification, so that He would be the firstborn the most beloved and honored among many believers. And those whom He predestined, He also called; and those whom He called, He also justified declared free of the guilt of sin; and those whom He justified, He also glorified raising them to a heavenly dignity."

–ROMANS 8:29-30 (AMP)

Speak These Words Over Your Life

I shall fulfill my God-given destiny. Regardless of what excuses or obstacles I have allowed to hold me back in the past, I choose, right now, to cast aside every weight and every hindrance and to wholeheartedly pursue the plans and purposes God has for my life. He has given me purpose in life and called me into a grand destiny; I will not doubt my purpose. My God shall provide the necessary resources, the favor, and the opportunities to fulfill all He has destined for my life. I will not give up on the dreams God has given me. I will keep my eyes fixed on Him and accomplish all the plans that God has for me.

Chapter 3

I Have a Hope

Contrary to what most people believe, when the Bible refers to the word "hope," it is not referring to wishful thinking. Biblical hope is a spiritual force—confident trust in God, believing without reservation that God is on your side and will see you through any situation. Hope is the foundation for faith. Hope is the expectation of a better tomorrow because you know God is with you and is willing and able to help you, sustain you, and provide a path to victory for you.

You may not have any idea how or when your life is going to improve, how or when your dreams are going to be accomplished, how or when your storm will cease, but hope knows that it will because God is faithful and He will not let His child fail.

God loves you so deeply that He made a promise to you—no matter how cruel life seems, He will be there by your side to be your Friend, to help you, to strengthen you, and to provide a way out. He is our hope, He is our future, and He is our guarantee. You can have faith in His love for you, His ability to help you, and His willingness to make a way on your behalf.

Even if you find yourself in a tough spot, whether it's a huge problem or a minor issue, God will turn even the worst situations around for you. He'll shelter you in the storms of life—not just to escape them and hide, but to gain strength and renew your hope. Hope will sustain you in the middle of life's greatest difficulties. God will give you patience to endure, strength to persevere, and courage to overcome whatever challenges you may be facing. He'll make a way when there seems to be no way out. So smile and let your heart overflow with hope because what's impossible with man is possible with God!

Scriptures

For whatever was written in earlier times was written for our instruction, so that through endurance and the encouragement of the Scriptures we might have hope *and* overflow with confidence in His promises.

–ROMANS 15:4 (AMP)

So it is impossible for God to lie for we know that his promise and his vow will never change! And now we have run into his heart to hide ourselves in his faithfulness. This is where we find his strength and comfort, for he empowers us to seize what has already been established ahead of time—an unshakeable hope! We have this certain hope like a strong, unbreakable anchor holding our souls to God himself. Our anchor of hope is fastened *to the mercy seat* which sits in the heavenly realm beyond the sacred threshold.

–HEBREWS 6:18-19 (TPT)

Now may God, the inspiration and fountain of hope, fill you to overflowing with uncontainable joy and perfect peace as you trust in him. And may the power of the Holy Spirit continually surround your life with his super-abundance until you radiate with hope!

–ROMANS 15:13 (TPT)

Speak These Words Over Your Life

My Hope is in God—not in myself, others, or in this world's system. He is my refuge, and He is my strength. He is my deliverer. He will never leave me or forsake me. He will sustain me and lift me up in troubled times. He is my hope. He encourages me, comforts me, and gives me peace through His Word and by the Holy Spirit. In the midst of adversity and difficulties, He gives me strength and courage to persevere. He loves me unconditionally, and He will never leave me to face the circumstances of life alone. In His promises, I find joy, peace, and hope.

Chapter 4

I Have Grace

Grace is a truly remarkable force. It is the action of, the all-inclusive demonstration of, and the immensely powerful representation of God's love for you.

God forgives you, loves you, and wants the best for you. His grace is how He displays that great love for you in your life. He sent Jesus to die on the cross so that He could give us grace! Its very purpose is to reunite you with your Father and to keep you there, free from the pressures of living a perfect life through your own acts of devotion and sacrifice.

God has put in your heart passions, desires, and dreams that He knew you could not accomplish on your own. Your high calling is to accomplish your dreams **with** Him. His grace is a source of strength for and a protector of that calling. It gives you influence with people, it provides opportunities for you, it eradicates anything that would try to disrupt and disconnect you from God, and if you do make a mistake and sin, then grace is also there to wipe your slate clean. There is nothing you have done or ever could do, there is not a sin in existence, that is more powerful than His grace. God doesn't want you living a life constantly aware of where you are falling short; He wants you to live a life fully aware of His love for you. Nobody is perfect, but God knew that so His grace makes up for all our imperfections and shortcomings.

Grace stands in the gap between the "you" that you want to be, and the "you" that you actually are through Jesus.

And His grace doesn't stop there! It digs deeper into your life, mending broken hearts, putting relationships back together, healing emotional scarring, and freeing you up from the weights you once carried! The best part about this wonderful display of God's affection is this simple truth: it's unmerited. If there were a way to earn it, then there would be a way to lose it. But God gives it to us freely, so take ahold and praise the Lord for His grace!

Scriptures

For it is by grace [God's remarkable compassion and favor drawing you to Christ] that you have been saved [actually delivered from judgment and given eternal life] through faith. And this [salvation] is not of yourselves [not through your own effort], but it is the [undeserved, gracious] gift of God; not as a result of [your] works [nor your attempts to keep the Law], so that no one will [be able to] boast or take credit in any way [for his salvation].

–EPHESIANS 2:8-9 (AMP)

But by the grace of God I am what I am, and his grace toward me was not in vain. On the contrary, I worked harder than any of them, though it was not I, but the grace of God that is with me.

–1 CORINTHIANS 15:10 (ESV)

And God is able to make all grace [every favor and earthly blessing] come in abundance to you, so that you may always [under all circumstances, regardless of the need] have complete sufficiency in everything [being completely self-sufficient in Him], and have an abundance for every good work and act of charity.

–2 CORINTHIANS 9:8 (AMP)

Speak These Words Over Your Life

I am thankful for the gift of God's grace in my life. I am immersed in His loving embrace through the display of His grace. His grace picks me up when I fall short, and it gives me hope to face tomorrow with confidence and courage. His grace is a constant reminder that God loves me unconditionally, and His forgiveness knows no bounds. His grace sustains me in times of adversity and difficulty. His grace encourages and strengthens me when faced with challenges in life. His grace inspires me and gives me hope.

His grace has put a smile on my face, peace in my mind, joy in my heart, and has given me the strength to accomplish my destiny on this earth.

Chapter 5

I Have an Advocate

The Bible tells us that when Jesus went back to heaven, He took His place at the right hand of God. He now lives to make intercession for us. Jesus is praying for you right now! How cool is that! He has become your Advocate.

An advocate is "a person who publicly supports or recommends a particular cause or policy, or a person who pleads on someone else's behalf." Your Advocate is revealed in 1 John 2:1:

"My dear children, I am writing this to you so that you will not sin. But if anyone does sin, we have an advocate who pleads our case before the Father. He is Jesus Christ, the one who is truly righteous" (NLT).

This is the very reason why when you pray to God, you end your prayer with, "in Jesus' name, amen." Your prayers don't have to be perfect because Jesus is, and when He hears what you're saying, He takes your heart and pleads your case to God for you. It's a sweet transition because Jesus knows precisely what you are going through. The Bible even says,

"For we do not have a High Priest who is unable to sympathize and understand our weaknesses and temptations, but One who has been tempted [knowing exactly how it feels to be human] in every respect as we are, yet without [committing any] sin." –Hebrews 4:15 (AMP)

That means He knows exactly what you are feeling and wants to help you with it. Before many of the miracles Jesus performed, the Bible notes that He had compassion on them. Jesus loves you and feels the pain you've been going through. So when you feel inadequate, like you have let God down too many times, you don't have enough faith, and you are wondering why your prayers would be answered because you don't know the right words to say, remember that you can pour out your heart before God. Jesus will fill in the gaps of all your inadequacies and lack of faith, and He reminds God of His Word. Praise the Lord for Jesus, our Advocate!

Scriptures

For there is one God, and one mediator between God and men, the man Christ Jesus.

–1 Timothy 2:5 (KJV)

For Christ has entered, not into holy places made with hands, which are copies of the true things, but into heaven itself, now to appear in the presence of God on our behalf.

–Hebrews 9:24 (ESV)

Just think how much more the blood of Christ will purify our consciences from sinful deeds so that we can worship the living God. For by the power of the eternal Spirit, Christ offered himself to God as a perfect sacrifice for our sins. That is why he is the one who mediates a new covenant between God and people, so that all who are called can receive the eternal inheritance God has promised them. For Christ died to set them free from the penalty of the sins they had committed under that first covenant.

–Hebrews 9:14-15 (NLT)

Speak These Words Over Your Life

Jesus is my Lord, my Savior, and my Advocate. He has taken His seat of authority at the right hand of God. He now lives to make intercession for me. He pleads my case before Father God. When I sin and fall short, it is through His blood that I am forgiven and made righteous. He was my substitute on the cross. He took my sins, shortcomings, and failures. It's not by works or anything that I have done, but by His blood, I have salvation and access to God's unconditional love. Jesus is my Advocate. He is my righteousness, He is my saving grace, and He is my friend! Praise the Lord for my Advocate!

Chapter 6

I Have an Inheritance

Congratulations! You have an inheritance. The Bible tells us that we are joint heirs with Jesus, children of the Most High God, and positioned to carry out His will on the earth as the heirs to His kingdom. With that title, you have been given an inheritance. No matter what your station in life or how unworthy you might feel, you have an inheritance. Not because you deserve it or have done anything to earn it—it is there because of what Jesus did *for you* out of God's great love for you.

Normally we equate inheritance to a sum of money that is left for us, and though the definition definitely encompasses money, it is not limited to the financial arena. Read these various ways "inherit" is defined, "receive (money, property, or a title) as an heir at the death of the previous holder." Another is, "derive (a quality, characteristic, or predisposition) genetically from one's parents or ancestors." And lastly, "receive or be left with (a situation, object, etc.) from a predecessor or former owner."

When God adopted you into His family, He gave you an inheritance. He gave you a title: "Child of God." He gave you His spirit to develop your character and disposition and to help cultivate a quality of life that you would truly enjoy. He gave you a situation in which you have access to your Father God at all times.

The Bible is full of promises and gifts just like these, that belong to you, His child. The Bible is God's personal letter to you; it is part of your inheritance. So read, discover, and enjoy what God has spoken to you and choose to accept the gifts He gave to you. Choose to accept the title, the quality of life, and the situation He gave you. Choose to accept the promise of abundant provision for every area of your life. Choose to accept strength for the storms of life. Choose to accept the peace that passes all understanding. Choose to accept deliverance from adversity. And the greatest of all, choose to accept salvation and eternal life— the ability to spend eternity with our Savior and Father God in heaven. Enjoy your inheritance!

Scriptures

In Him we also were made God's heritage (portion) *and* we obtained an inheritance; for we had been foreordained (chosen and appointed beforehand) in accordance with His purpose, Who works out everything in agreement with the counsel *and* design of His own will.

–Ephesians 1:11 (AMPC)

Knowing [with all certainty] that it is from the Lord [and not from men] that you will receive the inheritance which is your [real] reward. [The One Whom] you are actually serving [is] the Lord Christ (the Messiah).

–Colossians 3:24 (AMPC)

Celebrate with praises the God and Father of our Lord Jesus Christ, who has shown us his extravagant mercy. For his *fountain of* mercy has given us a new life—we are reborn to experience a living, energetic hope through the resurrection of Jesus Christ from the dead. We are reborn into a perfect inheritance that can never perish, never be defiled, and never diminish. It is promised and preserved forever in the heavenly realm for you!

–1 Peter 1:3-4 (TPT)

Speak These Words Over Your Life

I have an inheritance. I am an heir of Christ, and as His heir, I receive what He has left me. All the promises that His Word contains belongs to me. My inheritance includes eternal life and a personal relationship with Jesus. I receive my provision, health, and the wisdom He has given to me, and therefore I declare that I am healthy, wealthy, and wise. I receive His peace that passes understanding, the joy that will strengthen me, and the love that will remind me who I am and what I mean to Him. I declare I am peaceful, joyful, and loved. I inherited the title of "child of the living God," so I refuse to degrade myself by thinking wrong thoughts, behaving in an inappropriate manner, and letting any foul things come out of my mouth. My inheritance in God is untouchable by the enemy, it cannot decay, and it cannot change or lessen in its life-changing potency.

Chapter 7

I Have the Greater One

When you accepted Jesus as your personal Savior, Jesus said His Spirit came to live in you. Jesus said He would make His home in you, and He even refers to our body as a temple to house His Spirit, the Holy Spirit of God Himself. This is the *same* Spirit that empowered Jesus on this earth to walk in God's divine will and the same Spirit that raised Jesus from the dead! That same Spirit now lives in *you*. He is there to guide, comfort, encourage, and ultimately empower you to do God's will upon the earth.

Greater is He that is in you than he *(Satan and the powers of darkness)* that is in the World.

He's greater than any storm that could come. He's greater than any crisis you could face. He's greater than any power that could come against you. He's greater than any sickness and disease, and He is greater than lack and poverty.

There will be times when the pain is great, when the fear sucks the air out of the room, and you don't feel God is near. The midnight hour comes to all of us; we are not immune to the challenges of life just because we are Christians. You may not feel like the spirit of a conqueror lives in you, but go forward in faith anyway.

The Bible tells us, "Many are the afflictions of the righteous, but God delivers them out of them all."

Regardless of what you feel, God is with you and will see you through. So, when you are facing that impossible task, look yourself in the mirror and remind yourself that the undaunted and unconquerable Spirit of God is within you. So lean on the Greater One. Activate His help through speaking the Word of God, and trust in him with an unwavering heart! Stop comparing yourself to the giant of a problem you are faced with, and instead compare the problem to the giant of a God who lives within you. No matter how great the problem is, He is greater still.

Scriptures

And what agreement has the temple of God with idols? For you are the temple of the living God. As God has said: "I will dwell in them and walk among them. I will be their God, and they shall be my people."

–2 Corinthians 6:16 (NKJV)

My dear children, you come from God and belong to God. You have already won a big victory over those false teachers, for the Spirit in you is far stronger than anything in the world.

–1 John 4:4 (MSG)

What shall we then say to these things? If God be for us, who can be against us?

–Romans 8:31 (KJV)

If anyone acknowledges that Jesus is the Son of God, God lives in them and they in God. And so we know and rely on the love God has for us.

–1 John 4:15-16a (NIV)

Speak These Words Over Your Life

Greater is He that is in me than he that is in the world. He is greater than any crisis I might face. He is greater than any storm that may arise. He is greater than any problem or difficulty in my life. He gives me the strength, courage, and fortitude to overcome. He gives me wisdom and supernatural direction to pursue God's plan for my life with confidence.

God is for me, He is with me, and He is on my side. The Creator of the universe, the shaper of all things, and my personal Savior is living in me. I will not fear in times of trouble. I will not magnify my problems; I will magnify God. No weapon formed against me will prosper. When my strength and endurance have reached their limit, I will lean on the Greater One, knowing that His strength will carry me through.

Chapter 8

I Have a Protector

Every day there are reports of shootings, terrorist attacks, and unfathomable crimes committed against innocent people. Sickness and disease run rampant. Tragedy and peril seem to be lurking around every corner. If we are not careful, it is easy to become fearful and anxious about our safety and the safety of our loved ones.

But I have good news! Part of the benefits and privileges of being a Christian is God's promise of protection for us and our family. One of the greatest passages on God's promise of protection for you, His child, can be found in the 91st Psalm. Read it, let His promise fill your heart with confidence and peace. Release the power of His words in your life by speaking them over yourself and your family. As we truly make Him our refuge, we can depend on and trust in His protection.

"You who sit down in the High God's presence, spend the night in Shaddai's shadow, Say this: "God, you're my refuge. I trust in you and I'm safe! That's right—he rescues you from hidden traps, shields you from deadly hazards. His huge outstretched arms protect you—under them you're perfectly safe; his arms fend off all harm. Fear nothing—not wild wolves in the night, not flying arrows in the day, Not disease that prowls through the darkness, not disaster that erupts at high noon. Even though others succumb all around, drop like flies right and left, no harm will even graze you. You'll stand untouched, watch it all from a distance, watch the wicked turn into corpses. Yes, because God's your refuge, the High God your very own home, Evil can't get close to you, harm can't get through the door. He ordered his angels to guard you wherever you go. If you stumble, they'll catch you; their job is to keep you from falling. You'll walk unharmed among lions and snakes, and kick young lions and serpents from the path."
Psalm 91:1-13 (MSG)

Scriptures

But the Lord is faithful, and He will strengthen you setting you on a firm foundation and will protect *and* guard you from the evil *one*.

–2 THESSALONIANS 3:3 (AMP)

God is a safe place to hide, ready to help when we need him. We stand fearless at the cliff-edge of doom, courageous in seastorm and earthquake, Before the rush and roar of oceans, the tremors that shift mountains.

–PSALM 46:1-3 (MSG)

The Lord is my Shepherd to feed, to guide and to shield me, I shall not want.

–PSALM 23:1 (AMP)

Even though I walk through the sunless valley of the shadow of death, I fear no evil, for You are with me; Your rod to protect and Your staff to guide, they comfort *and* console me.

–PSALM 23:4 (AMP)

Speak These Words Over Your Life

My family and I walk in complete and total protection from harm, evil, danger, and accidents of any kind. I refuse to live in fear. I will not worry or become anxious regarding our safety because I put my trust and confidence in God. I purpose to make Him my refuge and enjoy the promise of safety that comes with that position. I know He will keep us safe from danger and destruction. I am sensitive to the voice of the Holy Spirit and quick to obey His direction regarding the safety and well-being of my family.

Chapter 9

I Have Peace

It seems like we are all continually searching for more peace in our lives. Our peace is under constant attack. The flow of text messages, emails, calls and more from friends, family, and people we don't even know; the daily grind of work and everyday living; and the challenges that life throws at us on a regular basis can stress us out to the point where there is no peace left in our lives.

But is peace just the lack of feeling stressed, tired, or anxious? Can it be gained by a quiet evening, reading a novel, or watching a favorite show on TV? Maybe temporarily, but that kind of peace is fleeting and dissipates the moment you step back into the real world. When Jesus left this earth after being resurrected, He said this:

"Peace I leave with you, my peace I give unto you: not as the world giveth, give I unto you. Let not your heart be troubled, neither let it be afraid." John 14:27

Our minds and emotions can't comprehend how we can be calm, cool, and collected in the middle of the craziness of life. This is not the world's fleeting peace gained from external leisure but rather an everlasting peace that comes from our trust in God. In Isaiah 26, God says, "I will keep them in perfect peace whose eyes are fixed on me."

If you need more peace in your life, then maybe you need to change where you are looking. Peace is not the absence of problems. Peace is the state of a child of God who is self-assured because of their faith in Him, which means you can be full of peace even in the middle of a major crisis. Your joy and peace of mind are never at the mercy of your circumstances. When you choose to look to God and trust Him to take care of you and sustain you, then the busyness of life will cease to overwhelm you and His peace will bring you to a state of calmness and joy that can only come from Him.

Worry, fear, and anxiety say, "What if…", but peace smiles and says, "God will."

Scriptures

"The Lord will give strength unto his people; the Lord will bless his people with peace."

–Psalm 29:11 (KJV)

"May the God of hope fill you with all joy and peace as you trust in him, so that you may overflow with hope by the power of the Holy Spirit."

–Romans 15:13 (NIV)

"Do not be anxious or worried about anything, but in everything [every circumstance and situation] by prayer and petition with thanksgiving, continue to make your [specific] requests known to God. And the peace of God [that peace which reassures the heart, that peace] which transcends all understanding, [that peace which] stands guard over your hearts and your minds in Christ Jesus [is yours]."

–Philippians 4:6-7 (AMP)

Speak These Words Over Your Life

I have peace that passes all understanding. I can face any problem or challenge
in my life without getting fretful, disturbed,
or anxious. I refuse to let fear run rampant in
my life. I refuse to let the busyness of
everyday life stress me out. I refuse to let the
constant pressures of this life push me to the
edge. And I refuse to fall victim to my own
thoughts and emotions. I will not be
distraught or frustrated when unexpected
glitches or difficulties pop up in my life. In
the midst of trying times, I will find rest and
peace in the presence of the Almighty. I will
not turn my eyes from God no matter the
intensity of the storm I find myself in, for He
is my source of peace. I will not become
agitated because of what other people say or
do. I will keep my mind at peace and my
heart steady when I am tempted to worry or
become fearful because I put my trust in
God. His peace gives me assurance that
everything will work out for my good.

Chapter 10

I Have the Holy Spirit

The Holy Spirit is the source of power and strength which Jesus operated in while here on the earth. After His resurrection, Jesus promised that God would send the Holy Spirit to live in us as our supernatural resource for every area of life. Many think the Holy Spirit is some mystical, mysterious force that is flighty and unpredictable.

This is not the case; the Bible specifically tells us the roles that the Holy Spirit fulfills in our lives. He works in us, for us, and through us to fulfill the plan of God in our lives.

He is our Helper, forever lending support to those who ask God for help.

He is the Spirit of God. Your body acts as a temple to house His presence, so your spirit can commune with God. God speaks to us, through His spirit, by revealing the truth of the Bible and by wisdom spoken to our hearts. Our ability to hear His voice is enhanced in our time spent with the Lord in prayer and worship.

He is our Comforter. When life gets tough, He'll take us to the words that God has spoken to you—words of love, words of affirmation, words of strength, words of freedom, and words of hope.

He's our Counselor, helping us navigate life. He guides us to a place of peace and joy using the Word of God as a map for finding balance between work, play, relationships, and rest. He'll supply you with wisdom and guidance.

The Holy Spirit is here to help us. Many have tried to live life fighting all its storms, all their impure desires, and all their problems by themselves when help is available to us. The Bible puts it like this in Romans 8:5-6:

"Those who think they can do it on their own end up obsessed with measuring their own moral muscle but never get around to exercising it in real life. Those who trust God's action in them find that God's Spirit is in them—living and breathing God! Obsession with self in these matters is a dead end; attention to God leads us out into the open, into a spacious, free life." (MSG)

Scriptures

But the Helper (Comforter, Advocate, Intercessor—Counselor, Strengthener, Standby), the Holy Spirit, whom the Father will send in My name [in My place, to represent Me and act on My behalf], He will teach you all things. And He will help you remember everything that I have told you.

–JOHN 14:26 (AMP)

Then Peter said unto them, Repent, and be baptized every one of you in the name of Jesus Christ for the remission of sins, and ye shall receive the gift of the Holy Ghost.

–ACTS 2:38 (KJV)

Don't you realize that your body is the temple of the Holy Spirit, who lives in you and was given to you by God? You do not belong to yourself.

–1 CORINTHIANS 6:19 (NLT)

Speak These Words Over Your Life

I have the Holy Spirit living in me. The same Spirit that raised Christ Jesus from the dead lives in me, revitalizing and infusing my body with strength. And the Holy Spirit is working in me and through me to fulfill God's plan for my life. He is my Helper, He is my Comfort, and He is my Guide. He reveals the truths and insights in God's Word. As I study and meditate on the Scriptures, He gives me wisdom and understanding. When I am facing a critical decision, He gives me wisdom, strength, and courage to face any adversity or challenge life sends my way.

Chapter 11

I Have Authority and Dominion

You have authority and dominion as God's representative on this earth. Jesus operated in divine authority on this earth because He did His miracles through God's direction. Jesus said in John the 14th chapter,

That He did and said nothing lest He heard His father say it first.

Consequently, when Jesus exercised His authority to perform God's will on the earth, He looked within and sought the words that God would have Him speak over His current situation. He spoke those words with faith in God and confidence in His position as God's representative.

According to God's ultimate plan of redemption for us, through the death and resurrection of Jesus Christ, we were saved and have become Christ's ambassadors, equipped with His authority and dominion. Jesus himself tells us,

"Behold, I have given you authority to tread on serpents and scorpions, and over all the power of the enemy, and nothing shall hurt you." Luke 10:19 (ESV)

This doesn't mean you should look for snakes to step on or put yourself in a dangerous situation to prove something. God gives us wisdom, and if there is a way to avoid calamity, then we need to exercise that wisdom. The reason for your authority is for your protection—you are never to be powerless or a victim of circumstances or subdued by the power of the enemy. You are to walk confidently in faith. We are equipped and empowered to operate as Jesus did; He even said in the 14th chapter of John,

"Whoever believes in me will also do the works that I do; and greater works than these will he do, because I am going to the Father."

This doesn't seem possible, and in fact if Jesus didn't say it, then it would be difficult to believe. But He *did* say it, so you need never to shirk in fear or doubt when faced with impossible odds because you are a child of the Most High God! Jesus has bestowed upon us power and authority to walk in dominion while on this earth.

So, activate your authority by speaking the words of God in faith over your circumstances. Be secure in your position, and remember your authority—then speak out His words with faith in and through the delegated authority of Jesus Christ.

Scriptures

Then God said, "Let us make man in our image, after our likeness. And let them have dominion over the fish of the sea and over the birds of the heavens and over the livestock and over all the earth and over every creeping thing that creeps on the earth."

–Genesis 1:26 (ESV)

Now you understand that I have imparted to you all my authority to trample over his kingdom. You will trample upon every demon before you and overcome every power Satan possesses. Absolutely nothing will be able to harm you as you walk in this authority.

–Luke 10:19 (TPT)

What are mere mortals that you should think about them, human beings that you should care for them? Yet you made them only a little lower than God and crowned them with glory and honor. You gave them charge of everything you made, putting all things under their authority

–Psalms 8:4-6 (NLT)

Speak These Words Over Your Life

As God's ambassador and representative on this earth, I have dominion and authority to walk in total victory. The enemy has no power to bring destruction or calamity to my life. I walk and live with bold and confident faith. I am a victor, not a victim. I have learned to rise above the adverse circumstances of life. I am a joint heir with Jesus and enjoy the rights and privileges promised to me in God's Word.

Chapter 12

I Have Provision

Let there be no mistake or misconception about God's love for you—your needs touches Him. He is not indifferent concerning your affairs. He loves you and cares about you. He wants you to live a blessed and fulfilled life. Being in lack is not God's will for your life.

If you are going through some financial challenges right now, don't be discouraged. This is not indicative of God's disapproval or His will. God wants you to be successful. Even if your poor choices are the reason you are experiencing financial difficulties, God hasn't given up on you, so ask for His forgiveness and move on in His mercy and grace. Then, read His promises concerning your provision, speak them over your life, and thank God for His help. Choose to look more at His Word and less at the bills and your bank account. Dwell on His provision instead of your lack. Magnify God instead of the problem. God is your

Father, so ask Him if there is anything you should be doing differently and He will guide you in the way you should go.

Your debt may be forgiven, you may get a promotion at work to cover the difference, you may have an idea that produces a profit for your family, or opportunities may present themselves for you to earn extra income. It's up to Him how your provision comes, but it's up to you to believe that it's coming. Hear Jesus' thoughts about God's provision from His own mouth:

"If God gives such attention to the appearance of wildflowers—most of which are never even seen—don't you think he'll attend to you, take pride in you, do his best for you? What I'm trying to do here is to get you to relax, to not be so preoccupied with getting, so you can respond to God's giving. People who don't know God and the way he works fuss over these things, but you know both God and how he works. Steep your life in God-reality, God-initiative, God-provisions. Don't worry about missing out. You'll find all your everyday human concerns will be met."

–Matthew 6:30-33 (MSG)

Scriptures

But my God shall supply all your need according to his riches in glory by Christ Jesus.

–Philippians 4:19 (KJV)

If you remain in Me and My words remain in you [that is, if we are vitally united and My message lives in your heart], ask whatever you wish and it will be done for you.

–John 15:7 (AMP)

The blessing of the Lord makes a person rich, and he adds no sorrow with it.

–Proverbs 10:22 (NLT)

The Lord is my shepherd, <u>I lack nothing</u>.

–Psalm 23:1 (NIV)

Now to Him Who, by (in consequence of) the [action of His] power that is at work within us, is able to [carry out His purpose and] do superabundantly, far over and above all that we [dare] ask or think [infinitely beyond our highest prayers, desires, thoughts, hopes, or dreams].

–Ephesians 3:20 (AMPC)

Speak These Words Over Your Life

The Lord is my Provider, and He will supply all my needs. He loves me, cares about me, and wants me to succeed in life. He wants me to have a blessed and fulfilled life. He gives me wisdom and insight on how to manage my finances successfully. He gives me favor concerning financial transactions. He gives me creative ideas on how to increase my income. I declare all my bills paid. My debts are being reduced and eliminated. I am a child of the Most High God. It is not His will for me to have lack or live under financial stress. He provides me with multiple streams of income. I declare I shall have more than enough money each month to cover all my obligations and plenty left over to give to the Kingdom and the welfare of others.

Chapter 13

I Have the Promise of Healing and a Long Life

Health and healing are available to every Christian. It is a gift from God! God is a good God, and He sent Jesus to the earth to save His kids—not just from spiritual death but also from physical pain and torment! Jesus never denied anyone healing in the Bible who asked Him for it. The Bible puts it like this in Acts: *"God anointed Jesus of Nazareth with the Holy Spirit and power, and how **he went around doing good and healing all** who were under the power of the devil, because God was with him."*

The Bible also says that Jesus is the same yesterday, today, and forever, which means He's still in the healing business. Jesus loves you very much and wants you to be healthy and whole so that you can live life to the fullest! He said it Himself in the 10th chapter of John:

*"The thief comes only to steal and kill and destroy; **I have come that they may have life, and have it to the full.**"*

God was with Jesus, and it was God through Jesus who caused the healing to manifest on this earth. It is God's will for you to be healed. There is a name that God was called in the Bible, "*Jehovah Rapha,*" which means,

"I am the God that Heals."

God is not the author of sickness and diseases; He is the healer of them. He gave us His Word, which is filled with faith, life, and the promise of healing. It is through His words that God sends His healing.

"He sent out his word and healed them, snatching them from the door of death." Psalm 107:20 (NLT)

His Word is alive, and there is life in it to heal you. If you will meditate on His words and believe in Him, then the same life that is in the Word of God will come into you.

"My child, pay attention to what I say. Listen carefully to my words. Don't lose sight of them. Let them penetrate deep into your heart, for they bring life to those who find them, and healing to their whole body." Proverbs 4:20-22 (NLT)

Let His words penetrate deep into your heart and accept the gift of life and healing in them!

Scriptures

He was despised and rejected—a man of sorrows, acquainted with deepest grief. We turned our backs on him and looked the other way. He was despised, and we did not care. Yet it was our weaknesses he carried; it was our sorrows that weighed him down. And we thought his troubles were a punishment from God, a punishment for his own sins! But he was pierced for our rebellion, crushed for our sins. He was beaten so we could be whole. He was whipped so we could be healed.

—Isaiah 53:3-5 (NLT)

"Are you weary, carrying a heavy burden? Then come to me. I will refresh your life, for I am your oasis.

—Matthew 11:28 (TPT)

He personally carried our sins in His body on the cross willingly offering Himself on it, as on an altar of sacrifice, so that we might die to sin becoming immune from the penalty and power of sin and live for righteousness; for by His wounds you who believe have been healed.

—1 Peter 2:24 (AMP)

Speak These Words Over Your Life

I call my body strong, healthy, healed, and whole, free from sickness and disease. I am full of divine life and vitality. I declare every system in my body operates precisely the way God designed it to. I declare every organ and gland in my body is healthy and whole and functions at maximum efficiency. I declare my bones are strong. I declare my body is free from growths, tumors, cysts, and cancers. I declare my blood is healthy and free from disease or unhealthy cells. My immune system is strong and resilient. My sight is strong, and my hearing is clear. The life of God in me sustains me and keeps me healthy.

Chapter 14

I Have a Way Out

Sometimes we may find ourselves in a situation where it looks like there is no way out. The problem is too big, the odds are stacked against us, and it seems like there is no way to climb out. Fear and worry may have driven you to discouragement and despair. But don't be dismayed, I have good news for you! With Jesus, there is always a way out. There is not a hole so deep that He is unable to pull you out of it! If you are lost and confused, He'll find you. If you are weary and tired, He'll strengthen you. If you are dry and broken, He'll refresh you and supply you.

He said it Himself: "I am the Way." He is your way out of every adverse circumstance. He is the way you break free from worry, fear, and depression. He is the way to a loving relationship with your Father, God. He is the way to eternal life. You have Him in your life as your Friend and Advocate! Instead of leaning on your own strength, lean on Him. Let His Word bolster your faith in Christ and spur you on towards victory.

It's not time to lie down; it's time to rise up! It's not time to withdraw; it's time to advance! It's not time to give up; it's time to fight back! Through His Word and the guidance of the Holy Spirit, He sets a path of deliverance before you. Ask God about your part and then trust Him to do what you can't. Whether the Lord delivers you "from" a trial or "through" a trial, know that He is with you to provide courage, strength, and endurance.

So, quit magnifying the problem and start magnifying the solution, Jesus Christ. Start thanking God for your deliverance right in the middle of your trial. There is no stronger proclamation of faith than thanksgiving for help while you see no signs of change.

So, keep believing, keep trusting in His promises to you, be willing to play your role in your deliverance, and you will see the other side of the trial.

Scriptures

"If you'll hold on to me for dear life,"
says God, "I'll get you out of any trouble. I'll
give you the best of care if you'll only get to
know and trust me. Call me and I'll answer,
be at your side in bad times; I'll rescue you,
then throw you a party. I'll give you a long
life, give you a long drink of salvation!"

–Psalm 91:14-16 (MSG)

For the Lord is the Spirit, and wherever
the Spirit of the Lord is, there is freedom.

–2 Corinthians 3:17 (NLT)

But I'll take the hand of those who don't
know the way, who can't see where they're
going. I'll be a personal guide to them,
directing them through unknown country. I'll
be right there to show them what roads to take,
make sure they don't fall into the ditch. These
are the things I'll be doing for them—sticking
with them, not leaving them for a minute."

–Isaiah 42:16 (MSG)

Jesus saith unto him, I am the way, the
truth, and the life: no man cometh unto the
Father, but by me.

–John 14:6 (KJV)

Speak These Words Over Your Life

I will not fear when I feel the pressures of this world constricting me, for I know that they cannot crush me. I will not fall into despair when I can't figure things out. I will not be anxious or intimidated; instead, I will put my trust in God. I know He will bring me out. I declare that there is no such thing as a hopeless situation with God. I will not panic when faced with what seems to be impossible odds, because I know that what is impossible with man is possible with God. I will not distress if I make a mistake or if a crisis arises because I know that with God there is always a way out. God gives me clarity of thought and wisdom to handle my situation. I'm never forsaken, never left to fend for myself, and never will I stand alone against the attacks of this world!

Chapter 15

I Have Faith

Faith is the key that opens the door to all of God's blessings, the catalyst that produces an environment for the miraculous to manifest in your life. Faith is essential to receiving what God has promised us. The Bible defines faith like this:

"Now faith is the assurance (the confirmation, the title deed) of the things we hope for, being the proof of things we do not see and the conviction of their reality. faith perceiving as real fact what is not revealed to the senses." (Hebrews 11:1 AMPC)

The Bible further tells us that God has given every believer *"a measure of faith."* This means you have the ability to believe in something you can't see but you know in your heart is true anyway. That's how you became a Christian! It is up to you to grow the faith you have been given. Growing your faith is simple—you have to feed it and exercise it.

You feed your faith by reading the Word of God. As you take time to get to know God personally through His Word, faith will come alive in your heart. When you read and meditate on God's promises, your faith will grow stronger and stronger. Your knowledge of who God is, what He has already done for you, and what He has promised will begin to expand. This process creates an intimacy with God that causes our faith in Him to flourish.

You exercise your faith by believing in what God said in His Word regardless of how adverse your circumstances are and then by activating the Word of God by speaking it over your life. When the Bible says one thing, and you are experiencing another thing, faith chooses to trust that your circumstances will conform to what the Bible says. Choose to focus on the Word of God more than your circumstance, choose to see that God is bigger than your problem, choose to speak His words instead of fear and doubt, and you have the guarantee of God that your circumstances will conform to what He has promised you.

Scriptures

Because of the grace that God gave me, I can say to each one of you: don't think of yourself more highly than you ought to think. Instead, be reasonable since God has measured out a portion of faith to each one of you.

–Romans 12:3 (CEB)

Now faith is the assurance (the confirmation, the title deed) of the things we hope for, being the proof of things we do not see *and* the conviction of their reality faith perceiving as real fact what is not revealed to the senses.

–Hebrews 11:1 (AMPC)

For whatsoever is born of God overcometh the world: and this is the victory that overcometh the world, even our faith.

–1 John 5:4 (KJV)

But without faith it is impossible to please him: for he that cometh to God must believe that he is, and that he is a rewarder of them that diligently seek him.

–Hebrews 11:6 (KJV)

Speak These Words Over Your Life

I have faith in God's Word. I put my trust and confidence in Him. I walk by faith and not by sight. I choose to trust in the Lord no matter what comes my way. Even in the midst of difficulties and challenges, I have faith that God will not let me down or abandon me. As I study and meditate on His words, my faith grows stronger and stronger. My faith is in God, not in my ability, not in others, and not in the government. It is only in my God. By faith, I will overcome any challenges life throws at me. By faith, I will fulfill God's purpose and destiny for my life.

Chapter 16

I Have Wisdom and Guidance

Our decisions define and shape our lives. Who you are today is the product of choices you have made in the past, and the choices you make today will decide your future. This is why it is so critical that we learn how to follow God's lead in our lives; it takes all the stress, fear, and anxiety out of our lives and replaces it with peace and purpose.

Being guided by God sounds mystical, as if you were going to hear a thundering voice from heaven that tells you what you need to do. It's much less spectacular than that but no less powerful. God leads us through wisdom and peace. His wisdom comes from three major sources: the leading of the Holy Spirit, His Word, and the godly counsel of others. The Bible says in Colossians,

"And let the peace (soul harmony which comes) from Christ rule (act as umpire

continually) in your hearts deciding and settling with finality all questions that arise in your minds, in that peaceful state to which as members of Christ's one body you were also called to live. And be thankful (appreciative), giving praise to God always."

When you trust God with your life and live in His peace, you'll be able to discern the best decision. God will provide you with wisdom if you just ask for it. The Bible puts it like this:

"If any of you lacks wisdom to guide him through a decision or circumstance, he is to ask of our benevolent God, who gives to everyone generously and without rebuke or blame, and it will be given to him."

If the wisdom is from God, we will have peace about acting upon that wisdom. God genuinely wants the best for your life. He wants you to be joyful, at peace, and full of confidence knowing that you are fulfilling the purpose that He has specifically chosen for you. So whether you have a big decision to make or a small one, lean on God for wisdom and guidance, because if it matters to you, it matters to Him.

Scriptures

"If any of you lacks wisdom [to guide him through a decision or circumstance], he is to ask of [our benevolent] God, who gives to everyone generously and without rebuke *or* blame, and it will be given to him."

–JAMES 1:5 (AMP)

"But the wisdom that comes from heaven is first of all pure; then peace-loving, considerate, submissive, full of mercy and good fruit, impartial and sincere."

–JAMES 3:17 (NIV)

And let the peace (soul harmony which comes) from Christ rule (act as umpire continually) in your hearts [deciding and settling with finality all questions that arise in your minds, in that peaceful state] to which as [members of Christ's] one body you were also called [to live]. And be thankful (appreciative), [giving praise to God always].

–COLOSSIANS 3:15 (AMPC)

Thus says the Lord, your Redeemer, the Holy One of Israel: "I am the Lord your God, who teaches you to profit, who leads you in the way you should go."

–ISAIAH 48:17 (ESV)

Speak These Words Over Your Life

By the Spirit of the Lord and through God's words, I receive His wisdom for every area of my life. By His Spirit, He leads and guides me in the fulfillment of His perfect will. He gives me direction and insight concerning any decisions I need to make. He gives me clarity of thought and discernment when faced with perplexing situations. He gives me sound and accurate judgement when considering options that require my input. I declare that because I walk in God's wisdom, His peace is the anchor for my soul.

Chapter 17

I Have Victory

Even though we are Christians, there is no question that we will face challenges and difficulties in life. The Bible even tells us that *"Many are the afflictions of the righteous but the Lord delivers them out of them all."*

You may get a few scrapes and bruises along the way, but if you trust in God, cling to His Word, and refuse to give into despair, you will overcome. Your situation might feel hopeless, and it might look like there is no way out, but with God's help you can and you will overcome anything!

Everyone's needs and desires are different. But whatever you specifically need to achieve your goals, to see your dreams realized, to overcome an addiction, or to make it through a crisis—whatever it may be—God is your answer.

God did not promise us that we would never have any problems in our lives, but He did promise us the victory over them. You may be knocked down by trouble, but with God's strength you can get back up again. You may feel perplexed or distraught, but there is no need to worry because God will give you the wisdom to see you through any situation. You may feel under pressure, but there is no need to be anxious when God is with you and for you.

God's will for your life is total victory— victory in every area of your life. Victory over the powers of darkness, victory over any adversity, and victory over any obstacle that would keep you from achieving your God-given destiny. The Bible tells us that through the Lord, we are more than conquerors—we are world overcomers.

Christ is living in you, and He overcame sin, all the power of the enemy, and even death itself! So, victory is part of your spiritual DNA. God created you by and for complete and total victory! Let go of your fear, worry, and anxiety and let Him strengthen you, encourage you, and lead you in His peace to a place of victory.

With God, your future is secure and your victory assured.

I HAVE VICTORY

Scriptures

But thanks be to God! He gives us the victory through our Lord Jesus Christ.

–1 CORINTHIANS 15:57 (NIV)

Now thanks be unto God, which **always** causeth us to triumph in Christ, and maketh manifest the savour of his knowledge by us in every place.

–2 CORINTHIANS 2:14 (KJV)

We are hedged in (pressed) on every side troubled and oppressed in every way, but not cramped *or* crushed; we suffer embarrass-ments *and* are perplexed *and* unable to find a way out, but not driven to despair; We are pursued (persecuted and hard driven), but not deserted to stand alone; we are struck down to the ground, but never struck out *and* destroyed;

–2 CORINTHIANS 4:8-9 (AMPC)

Speak These Words Over Your Life

I have the victory!!! I am a champion of God, I am a child of the Most High, I am an ambassador for His Kingdom, I have Jesus Christ as my advocate, and I have a portion of the same spiritual substance that God used to frame the world: Faith, both as a shield and a sword to protect and fight back against any and all attacks of the enemy.

I am strong in the Lord and the power of His might. I am a victor, not a victim. I am more than a conqueror through my Lord Jesus Christ. I am a world overcomer. I will arise above every challenge that confronts me. I will boldly and confidently meet every adversity with undaunted faith.

My victory is as sure as the Word of God, which is my foundation. I will run my race, reach the goals God has put before me, fulfill my calling, and I shall have victory in every area of my life.

Chapter 18

I Have the Armor of God

You alone are not strong enough to withstand all the problems and trials that you face in life by yourself. That is why God makes His armor available to every Christian. It is His answer to the attacks of the enemy. It is up to you to wear it and use it!

You fasten the Belt of Truth by allowing the Word of God to be the final authority in your life—by living your life according to its principles, by transforming your words, actions, and by conforming your very perspective to the Word of God. The Bible is truth, and by using it as your belt, you hold the rest of your armor in the correct place.

You equip the Breastplate of Righteousness by accepting Jesus' sacrifice as a sufficient punishment for any mistake you've made—or will make. You protect the love in your heart by accepting His great love for you, which negates your enemy's attempt at condemnation.

Strap on your feet the shoes of the Gospel of Peace. They give you firm footing and stability in the Spirit, allowing you to advance through life in the Lord's strength and not your own, with your eyes firmly fixed on the Lord. God said, "I will keep him in perfect peace whose mind is fixed on me."

Raise your Shield of Faith by choosing to look at God's Word instead of the circumstances in your life. Walk by faith, and not by sight. Raise the shield by choosing to unwaveringly trust in God, knowing He will never leave you or forsake you. He shall deliver you from all the attacks of the enemy!

Put on the Helmet of Salvation. You have been saved from a life fated for destruction and have been adopted into the kingdom of light and have access to all the rights and privileges that go with that position, so recognize that Jesus' sacrifice is your salvation. He died and rose again so that God could remake you from head to toe.

And finally, draw your Sword of the Spirit! It's God's Spirit of dynamite power, which is the spoken Word of God. Face every adversity with the confidence and determination of a conqueror who has the assurance of total victory!

Scriptures

¹³ Therefore put on God's complete armor, that you may be able to resist *and* stand your ground on the evil day [of danger], and, having done all [the crisis demands], to stand [firmly in your place].

¹⁴ Stand therefore [hold your ground], having tightened the belt of truth around your loins and having put on the breastplate of integrity *and* of moral rectitude *and* right standing with God,

¹⁵ And having shod your feet in preparation [to face the enemy with the firm-footed stability, the promptness, and the readiness produced by the good news] of the Gospel of peace.

¹⁶ Lift up over all the [covering] shield of saving faith, upon which you can quench all the flaming missiles of the wicked [one].

¹⁷ And take the helmet of salvation and the sword that the Spirit wields, which is the Word of God.

–Ephesians 6:13-18 (AMPC)

Speak These Words Over Your Life

I have the spiritual armor of God at my disposal. I choose to put on my armor today. I am more than a conqueror, and I can do all things through Christ who strengthens me. With God's armor on, I am invincible. I am ready for anything and equal to anything that life throws my way. By His Spirit and through His Word I shall be victorious in every challenge I face. God's Word is the final authority in my life. Its truth and principles are my foundation and protect my heart. I will govern my thoughts and actions according to its direction. I know that Jesus' sacrifice assures my forgiveness and wipes the slate clean and I have now been redeemed from sin and the destructive forces of evil. I will advance in life with His peace leading the way. I will not be moved by what I see or deterred by what I feel; instead I will walk by faith, trusting in God's unfailing love and faithfulness. God's armor equips me with all I need to live a life of victory and fulfill my God-given destiny.

If you would like to accept Jesus as your personal Savior then pray this prayer:

Heavenly Father,

I come to You now in the precious name of Your Son, Jesus. You said in Your Word that if I confess with my mouth, "Jesus is Lord," and believe in my heart that God has raised Him from the dead, I will be saved. So, Father, right now, I ask that your forgive me of all my sins and I confess that Jesus is my Lord and my Savior. Jesus, I ask You to come into my heart right now. Thank You Lord. I am saved. Amen.

Other books by Jake & Keith

Keep Calm & Trust God (Vol. 1)

Keep Calm & Trust God (Vol. 2)

Keep Calm Gift Edition (Vol. 1 & 2)

Scriptural Prayers for Victorious Living

Let Not Your Heart Be Troubled

I Am What the Bible Says I AM